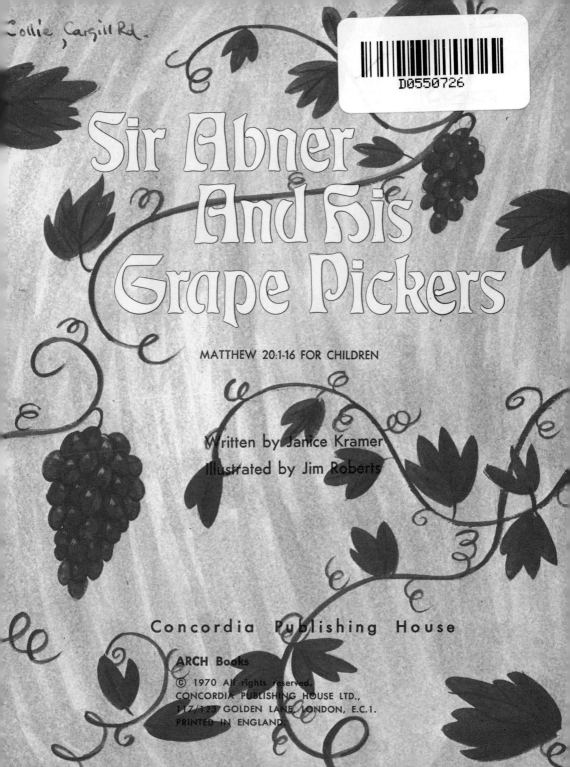

Sir Abner And His Grape Pickers

MATTHEW 20:1-16 FOR CHILDREN

Written by Janice Kramer
Illustrated by Jim Roberts

Concordia Publishing House

ARCH Books

© 1970 All rights reserved.
CONCORDIA PUBLISHING HOUSE LTD.,
117/123 GOLDEN LANE, LONDON, E.C.1.
PRINTED IN ENGLAND.

Sir Abner was sleeping
as sound as a rock.
He woke with a jerk
when he heard someone knock.
"Who is it?" he called
with a stretch and a yawn.
"Who's waking me up
at the hour of dawn?"

"It's Hector, your helper,"
the timid voice said.
"Oh, please, sir, get up
and get out of bed.
The grapes in the vineyard
are ready to fall.
We need to have workers
to harvest them all."

Sir Abner got dressed
in a hurry and then
went out and found
twenty-five healthy young men.
"I'll pay you one silver,"
he said to each one,
"to work in my vineyard
until the day's done."

"That's fine," said the men
as they quickly agreed.
"One silver is very
good wages indeed.

We'll carry in all
that your vineyard can yield."
And off they went running
to Sir Abner's field.

The morning soon passed.
It was time to eat lunch.
But just as Sir Abner
was starting to munch,
he heard a knock-knock
on the dining room door.
"Who is it?" he cried
with a great hungry roar.
"It's Hector, your helper,"
the timid voice said.
"Oh, please, sir, put down
your roast beef and your bread.
The vines are so full,
and there's so much to do.
We need some more workers
to add to our crew!"

So out to the street
went Sir Abner again.
He looked in the market
and found some more men.
"I promise," he told them,
"to give you good pay
to work in my vineyard
the rest of the day."

"That's fine," said the men.
"We'll do all that we can."
And off to the vineyards
they willingly ran.

By this time Sir Abner
was weary indeed.
"I'll go take a bath!"
he cried. "That's what I need!"

Sir Abner went home
to get into the tub.
But just as he started
to rub and to scrub,
he heard a knock-knock
on the door of the bath.
"Who is it?" he shouted,
his heart filled with wrath.

"It's Hector, your helper,"
the timid voice said.
"Oh, please take a towel
and dry off your head.
Unless we find more men
to work right away,
we'll never be able
to finish today."

Sir Abner was not
very happy just then.
He dressed and went out
and found thirteen more men.
"There's only one hour,"
he said, "before night.
Go work in my vineyard.
I'll pay you what's right."

"That's fine," said the men.
"We won't dawdle or shirk."
They ran to the vineyard
and started to work.

"And now," sighed Sir Abner,
"Perhaps I can dare
to go take a nap
in my favourite chair!"

He hurried on home
and unbuckled his shoes.
No sooner, it seemed,
had he started to snooze
when he heard a knock-knock
on the door of the room.
"I know who that is,"
sighed Sir Abner with gloom.

"Hector?" he shouted.
The voice answered, "Yes!
Now, how in the world, sir,
did you ever guess?

I just came to tell you
we're done for the day.
The workers are waiting
out here for their pay."

Sir Abner got out
his big strong money box
that needed six keys
to undo all the locks.

"Let's see, now," he mumbled.
"One silver for you,
for you, and for you,
and for you there too!"

Before old Sir Abner
was finally done,
he handed one silver
to every last one.

"But, sir," cried the men
who had laboured all day,
"we think that we ought
to be getting more pay!
We've worked very hard
in your vineyard since dawn.
The rest of these fellows
came much later on!"

"That fact," said Sir Abner,
"I cannot protest.
I know that you've worked
more today than the rest.

"But when you were hired,
you quickly agreed
one silver was very
good wages indeed!
You have what I promised you.
Why should you care
what I pay these other men?
That's my affair!"

The men were content.
They went to buy meat
and raisins and bread
for their children to eat.
"Well done, sir!" cried Hector.
"You did what was right!
Now with your permission
I bid you goodnight!"

"If Hector's in bed,"
thought Sir Abner with glee,
"there's no one around
to come bothering me."
He ran to his room
and with one mighty leap
jumped under the covers
and fell fast asleep.

DEAR PARENTS:

The author has written a delightful story by using her vivid imagination, but the basic elements are faithful to Jesus' kingdom parable in Matthew 20:1-16.

Jesus addressed this parable to the Pharisees and others who resembled the grumblers in the story. The Pharisees, who thought they were in a better class, were offended because Jesus was a companion of lowly outcasts and despised sinners. In this story Jesus makes a special point of God's kindness to all people.

The vineyard owner had compassion on the unemployed workers. Men who received no pay would not have bread for their hungry children. The small pay for an hour's work would not feed a family. Pity for these poor men who picked grapes for only an hour moved the owner to give them a full day's wages. The parable describes not an arbitrary action but the kind act of a generous man who is full of sympathy for the poor.

And that is how God deals with men. He is merciful. Even to great sinners and lowly outcasts He grants a place in His kingdom. No one is good enough to earn a position; God gives His kingdom because He is good and gracious. Everyone receives His kingdom by faith alone.

We suggest that you talk to your child about the goodness and generosity of the vineyard owner. Use the story to point to the greater kindness of God, who gives Jesus Christ as the Saviour of all sinners in the whole world. Turn your child away from all proud and odious comparisons, and point him to the gracious kindness of God toward us all in Christ Jesus.

THE EDITOR